# CENTER ICE
## The Stanley Cup

**Jaime Winters**

CRABTREE
Publishing Company
www.crabtreebooks.com

ROUND LAKE AREA
LIBRARY
906 HART ROAD
ROUND LAKE, IL 60073
(847) 546-7060

**Author:** Jaime Winters

**Publishing plan research and development:**
Reagan Miller, Crabtree Publishing Company

**Editors:** Marcia Abramson, Kelly Spence

**Proofreader:** Wendy Scavuzzo

**Photo research:** Melissa McClellan

**Cover Design:** Samara Parent

**Design:** T. J. Choleva

**Prepress technician:** Samara Parent

**Print and production coordinator:**
Katherine Berti

**Consultant:**
Ross Firmin, Hamilton Minor Hockey Council

Developed and produced for Crabtree Publishing
by BlueAppleWorks Inc.

Image on cover: Los Angeles Kings Captain
Dustin Brown hoists the Stanley Cup after
winning the 2014 Championship.

Image on title page: Patrick Kane celebrates after
Chicago Blackhawks win the Cup in 2013.

**Illustrations:** Carlyn Iverson (p 21 bottom, p 28 left)

**Photographs:**
**Front Cover:** Icon Sports Media: Chris Williams
**Interior: Shutterstock.com:** © Daniel M. Silva (TOC); © B Calkins (page toppers);
© Shooter Bob Square Lenses (hand & puck); © Kuco (p 8–9 top); © Christopher
Penler (p 12–13 top, p 20–21 top, p 20 bottom, p 26–27 bottom); © Scott Prokop (p 21
middle); © Litwin Photography (p 26–27 top); **Bigstock.com:** © iwantitall (p 14 left)
**Public Domain:** Bachrach44 (p 5 top); Alexander Henderson (p 6 right); Topley
Studio Fonds (p 6 left, 7 right); Conn Smythe Fonds (p 8–9 bottom); p. 8 left; p. 8
right; W.J. Gage & Co. (p 9 right); p. 9 left; Samuel J. Jarvis/Library and Archives
Canada/PA-025056 (p. 10); p 11 left; p. 12 bottom, left; Weekend Magazine/Louis
Jaques/Library and Archives Canada/e002505651 (p 16 left); Weekend Magazine/
Louis Jaques/Library and Archives Canada/e002505659 (p 16 middle); Jaques,
Louis/Library and Archives Canada/e002343728 (p 16 right); Weekend Magazine/
Louis Jaques/Library and Archives Canada/e002505660 (p 19 left); United States
Marine Corps photo by Pfc. Christopher D. Lyttle (p 25 bottom); hockeymedia.
ca/Richard Scott (p 29 right bottom); **Keystone Press:** © AB5 (title page); © Louis
Lopez (p 4); © Kostas Lymperopoulos (p 13 bottom, p 15 left); © Patrick Green (p
14 bottom); © Dirk Shadd (p 15 right); © Gerry Angus (p 15 middle); © Detroit Free
Press (p 17); © Robert B. Shaver (p 20 left); © Chris Williams/Icon Smi (p 27 left);
**Zumapress.com:** © Perry Mah/Edmonton Sun/Qmi Agenc (p 23 top); © Bob Fina
(p 23 bottom); **Creative Commons:** Ian Muttoo( p 5 bottom); Scazon (p 7 left);
Michael Miller (p 14 right); Scorpion0422 (p 19 right); Charny (p 22); Andy (p 25 top);
Genevieve2 ( p 28 right, p 29 top); Allie from Vancity (p 29 left) © Stephen Wise (p 30)

**Library and Archives Canada Cataloguing in Publication**

Winters, Jaime, author
    Center ice : the Stanley Cup / Jaime Winters.

(Hockey source)
Includes index.
Issued in print and electronic formats.
ISBN 978-0-7787-0758-5 (bound).--ISBN 978-0-7787-0707-3 (pbk.).--
ISBN 978-1-4271-7681-3 (pdf).--ISBN 978-1-4271-7677-6 (html)

    1. Stanley Cup (Hockey)--Juvenile literature. I. Title.

GV847.7.W56 2014        j796.962'648        C2014-903832-1
                                            C2014-903833-X

**Library of Congress Cataloging-in-Publication Data**

Winters, Jaime, author.
    Center Ice : The Stanley Cup / Jaime Winters.
        pages cm. --  (Hockey source)
    Includes index.
    ISBN 978-0-7787-0758-5 (reinforced library binding) --
    ISBN 978-0-7787-0707-3 (pbk.) -- ISBN 978-1-4271-7681-3 (electronic pdf.)
    -- ISBN 978-1-4271-7677-6 (electronic html.)
    1. Stanley Cup (Hockey)--Juvenile literature. 2. Hockey--Juvenile
    literature.  I. Title.

    GV847.7.W55 2015
    796.962'648--dc23
                            2014029473

# Crabtree Publishing Company

www.crabtreebooks.com        1-800-387-7650

Printed in the U.S.A./092014/JA20140811

Copyright © **2015 CRABTREE PUBLISHING COMPANY**. All rights reserved. No part of this publication may be reproduced,
stored in a retrieval system or be transmitted in any form or by any means, electronic, mechanical, photocopying, recording,
or otherwise, without the prior written permission of Crabtree Publishing Company. In Canada: We acknowledge the financial
support of the Government of Canada through the Canada Book Fund for our publishing activities.

**Published in Canada**
Crabtree Publishing
616 Welland Ave.
St. Catharines, ON
L2M 5V6

**Published in the United States**
Crabtree Publishing
PMB 59051
350 Fifth Avenue, 59th Floor
New York, New York 10118

**Published in the United Kingdom**
Crabtree Publishing
Maritime House
Basin Road North, Hove
BN41 1WR

**Published in Australia**
Crabtree Publishing
3 Charles Street
Coburg North
VIC 3058

# TABLE OF CONTENTS

## LET'S PLAY HOCKEY!

# THE ULTIMATE CUP

No trophy in the pro sports world is as tough to win as the Stanley Cup. Why is the quest for the Cup so **grueling**? How did the National Hockey League (NHL) trophy become so famous? And how did the Cup become a breakfast bowl of champions?

## Cup of Dreams

Each year, NHL players dream of winning the Stanley Cup. They play 82 games in the regular season, scrapping, elbowing, and **body checking** for playoff spots. It's all for a chance to face off for the Cup. The team that wins the playoffs wins the Cup—and all the glory that comes with it. The winners' names are engraved on one of the silver bands attached to the bottom. Is it any wonder that every player's **ultimate** dream is to hoist the Cup?

*Right wing Justin Williams of the Los Angeles Kings celebrates with the Stanley Cup after his team defeated the New York Rangers in the 2014 NHL Finals.*

## Who's Stanley?

No, Stanley is not the owner of the Cup. Neither is the NHL. The Stanley Cup is named after Lord Stanley of Preston. Lord Stanley was the Governor General of Canada in 1892. He donated the Cup as a trophy to be won by the top **amateur** hockey team in the **Dominion** of Canada. Lord Stanley called it the Dominion Hockey Challenge Cup. He entrusted two people to care for and **govern**, or control, the Cup. These people are called trustees. Today, the NHL has an agreement with the trustees to take care of the Cup.

## Not One But Three Stanley Cups!

There are actually three Cups used for different jobs. The original bowl was retired after 71 years, and is on display at the Hockey Hall of Fame. In 1963, a new Presentation Cup was created and, in 1993 a **replica**, or exact copy, of the Presentation Cup was made. The replica Cup stands in for the Presentation Cup at the Hockey Hall of Fame when the Presentation Cup is on the road.

### Cool Fact!

In 1893, the Montreal Hockey Club became the first team to win the Cup. In 1993, the Montreal Canadiens won the Cup for a record-setting 24th time.

*Fans can see the Stanley Cup at the Hockey Hall of Fame in Toronto, Ontario. There are also exhibits about players, teams, and the NHL.*

# LORD STANLEY

Hockey **evolved** from early ball-and-stick games played around the world. In the 1200s, people in Ireland played hurling, a sport which used curved tree branches to hurl a cow dropping into an opponent's goal. By 1877, a student in Montreal had written down the first rules of hockey. Players across Canada followed the rules and hockey's popularity grew. In 1883, the Montreal Winter Carnival held the first hockey tournament.

Lord Arthur Frederick Stanley became a hockey fan after seeing his first game at the Montreal Winter Carnival.

## Family Falls for Hockey

Lord Stanley of Preston was a big fan of sports. In 1888, he became the Governor General of Canada. He and his family moved to Canada from England. Soon after, they watched their first hockey game at the Montreal Winter Carnival and fell

head over heels in love with hockey. Lord Stanley had a rink flooded at their house in Ottawa and his sons and daughter Isobel took up the game. In 1892, Lord Stanley bought a silver punch bowl and donated it as a prize to be won by the best amateur hockey team in Canada.

*Lord Stanley shelled out about $50 for this silver bowl, intended to hold punch. He had "Dominion Hockey Challenge Cup" engraved on one side and "From Stanley of Preston" on the other.*

## First Lady of Hockey

Lord Stanley's 14-year-old daughter Isobel became an avid fan and player of the game. She founded the first women's hockey team. She also had a strong voice in convincing her father to create a trophy for amateur hockey. Her married name was Isobel Gathorne-Hardy. In 2002, an award was named after her. It honors female hockey players for service and leadership.

*Isobel Stanley, like her father, fell in love with hockey. She was one of the first women to play in a hockey game.*

# THE CHALLENGE TROPHY

The Cup was won for the first time in 1893. The only problem was that the winners didn't show up to accept it! The Montreal Hockey Club was arguing with its league about how things were run. Montreal skipped the ceremony in protest. So the league secretly accepted the Cup on their behalf.

*The Montreal Hockey Club won the first Stanley Cup. Their name was later changed to the Canadiens, but they kept their tradition of winning. In 1956-60, they set a new record with five **consecutive**, or continuous, Stanley Cup wins. This record has never been broken by any other team.*

## Cool Fact!

Lord Stanley never presented his Cup to any champions or even saw a game for it. When his brother fell ill in 1893, he had to return to England.

## Challengers Line Up

By the late 1800s, many hockey leagues had sprung up across Canada. According to the Challenge Cup rules, any league champions could challenge the Cup champion for the Cup at any time during the season. In 1894,

*Early hockey matches were played at Montreal's Victoria Skating Rink. No boards stood between the ice and the crowd in the rink. The rink was built for skating, not hockey.*

Ottawa challenged Montreal. Five thousand fans jammed into Montreal's Victoria Skating Rink for the game. Montreal won 3 to 1. Fans carried the champs out of the rink on their shoulders and the winners' names were the first to be engraved on the Cup. Soon, challengers began lining up to play for the Cup. One year, teams battled for the Stanley Cup four times!

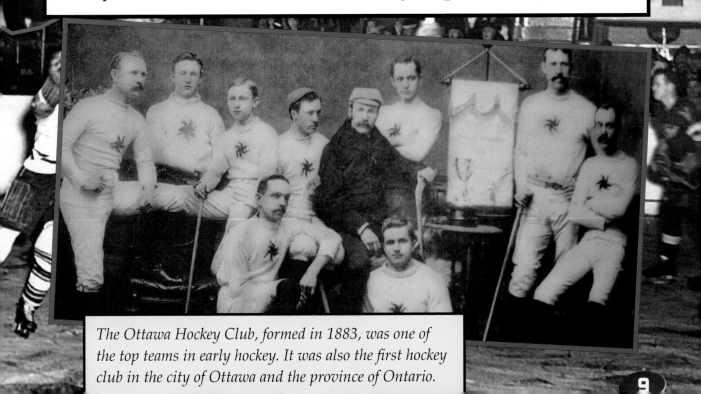

*The Ottawa Hockey Club, formed in 1883, was one of the top teams in early hockey. It was also the first hockey club in the city of Ottawa and the province of Ontario.*

# THE RISE OF THE NHL

Lord Stanley gave the Cup as a prize for amateur hockey in Canada. But as hockey players turned from amateur to pro, and leagues expanded into the United States, they didn't give up the Cup. They carried the Cup right along with them.

## The Cup Well Traveled

Challenges for the Cup were decided by the outcome of one game, the most goals in two games, or the most wins in three games. Since any league champions could call a challenge, the Cup changed hands from league to league, criss-crossing Canada. On the way, some leagues **folded**, some joined together, and some formed again.

*Trains were the only way for hockey teams to travel long distances in the early days of the sport. There were no team buses or airplanes back then! Players sometimes spent many days on a train just to get to the next game.*

## Challenges Scrapped

In 1915, the Cup trustees, the National Hockey Association (NHA) in the east, and the Pacific Coast Hockey Association (PCHA) in the west, **axed** the challenges. They agreed that the east and west champions would face off for the Cup in an end-of-season series. In 1917, the NHA folded and the National Hockey League (NHL) rose in its place. In 1924, the NHL expanded into the U.S. and the PCHA folded. By 1926, the NHL was the only league left on the ice.

*The first U.S. team to join the NHL was the Boston Bruins.*

*Many early NHL teams relied on strong defense. George Hainsworth, the Canadiens' goalie, set a record that still stands with 22 shutouts in 44 games in 1928-29.*

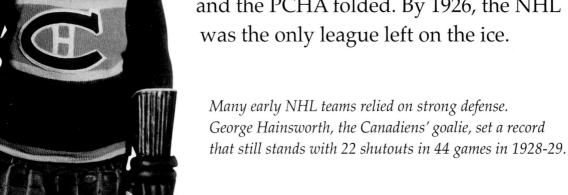

## Cup Crosses the Border

The Seattle Metropolitans joined the PCHA in 1915. Two years later, they became the first U.S. team to win the Cup. They beat the Montreal Canadiens three games to one. Montreal was stunned. The team had been so sure that they would win, they didn't even bring the Cup to the game!

# HOW THE NHL WORKS

Once challenges for the Cup were eliminated and the NHL became the only league in North America, only NHL teams were allowed to compete for hockey's top prize. All games were also played following NHL rules.

## Rules That Changed Every Game

Before challenges for the Cup were scrapped in 1915, the top teams from the east and west leagues played a best-of-five game series. Whichever team won the most games, won the Cup. Since the rules of the game differed between leagues, the rules of the game switched during the series. One game was played by one league's rules and the next game by the other league's rules.

*Joe Malone, a center for Montreal, was one of the first NHL stars. He scored 44 goals in 20 games, including five on the league's opening night.*

## The NHL Takes Over

Today, NHL rules determine which teams battle for the Cup. The NHL divides teams into two groups, called the eastern and western **conferences**. Each conference is split into three divisions. The top team in each division goes to the playoffs. After that, the five teams in each conference with the best records also get to compete for the Cup. The 16 teams play best-of-seven game series. The winner of each series advances to the next playoff round until only two teams are left. These teams face off in a final series of games for the Cup.

### Cool Fact!

In 1929, the Boston Bruins and New York Rangers met in the first Stanley Cup final between two U.S. teams. Boston beat New York, two games to zero in the series, winning the team's first Cup.

*Winning the Cup is the goal of all 30 NHL teams, as they battle through the 82 games of the regular season.*

# THE ORIGINAL SIX

The NHL started with five teams in 1917 and grew to 10 teams. But when the **Stock Market Crash** of 1929 triggered the **Great Depression**, many people fell on hard times. Money and jobs became scarce and several teams folded. By 1943, the NHL had only six teams: the Boston Bruins, Chicago Black Hawks, Detroit Red Wings, Montreal Canadiens, New York Rangers, and Toronto Maple Leafs. These teams became known as the **Original Six**.

THE ORIGINAL SIX – BOSTON BRUINS

THE ORIGINAL SIX – CHICAGO BLACK HAWKS

THE ORIGINAL SIX – DETROIT RED WINGS

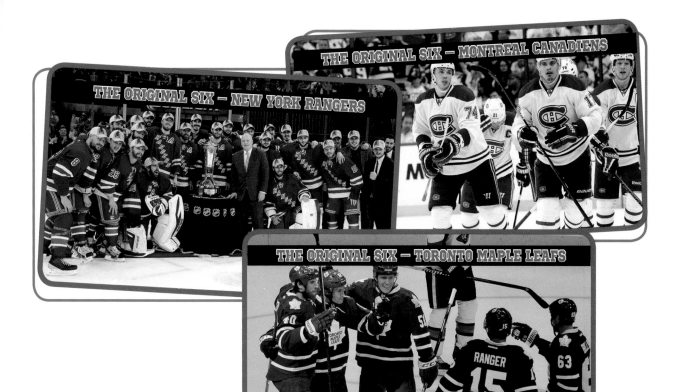

THE ORIGINAL SIX — NEW YORK RANGERS

THE ORIGINAL SIX — MONTREAL CANADIENS

THE ORIGINAL SIX — TORONTO MAPLE LEAFS

## The Dynasties

Over the next 25 years, the Original Six fought tooth and stick for the Cup. Since there were so few teams, the same teams faced each other in the Stanley Cup finals again and again. Soon, fierce **rivalries**, or competitions, grew between them. Many teams were stacked with hockey's top players. This led to **dynasties**—strings of players on the same team who dominated the game. The Detroit Red Wings, for example, finished first in the regular season for seven seasons in a row, from 1948-1955. No team has ever been able to do that since.

## Cool Fact!

When the Detroit Red Wings won the Cup in 1950, "Terrible" Ted Lindsay grabbed the Stanley Cup and lifted it high over his head. He wanted people to see what they had fought so hard to win. As he skated around the rink, a tradition was born!

# DYNAMITE DYNASTIES

Each dynasty of the Original Six had its own character. In the mid-1940s, the Toronto Maple Leafs rarely finished first in the regular season. They played their best in the playoffs. From 1947–1957, the Detroit Red Wings ruled the league with superstars. In 1950, the three players on Detroit's top-scoring line, known as "The Production Line," placed first, second, and third in the NHL for scoring. In the late 1950s, the Montreal Canadiens were loaded with talented players who practically owned the Cup.

*Center Henri Richard (left), goalie Jacques Plante (center), and left wing Dickie Moore (right) helped Montreal rule the NHL from 1956 to 1960. Richard won 11 Cups during his career— a record that still stands.*

## Dynasties Rule the Cup

From 1942-1967, the Cup left the hands of the NHL dynasties only once. And once a dynasty got hold of the Cup, it was tough to break its grip. The Toronto Maple Leafs won the Cup five times in seven seasons. The Red Wings took home the Cup four times in seven seasons, while the Canadiens won a record-setting five times in a row. Is it any wonder they were **archrivals**? When Toronto and Montreal met in the 1951 Stanley Cup finals, they battled so hard that each game of the series went into overtime. Only then did Toronto emerge with the Cup.

*Among U.S. teams, the Red Wings have won the most Stanley Cups with 11 NHL championships. Montreal has the most Cups, with 24, and Toronto has 13. No other team has 10 or more.*

## Where the Cup Belongs

The Chicago Black Hawks won the Cup in 1961. It was the year after Montreal had set their record with five Cup wins. One Montreal fan was so upset, that he stole the Cup out of a display case in the Chicago arena. When a police officer caught him in the act, the fan said, "I want to take it back where it belongs, to Montreal."

# THE EXPANSION ERA

In 1967, the expansion era began. Six new teams joined the NHL: the Los Angeles Kings, Minnesota North Stars, California Seals, Philadelphia Flyers, Pittsburgh Penguins, and St. Louis Blues.

## Set Up for the Cup

The new teams picked players from the Original Six in a special **draft**. However, the Original Six got to keep 11 of their players from being drafted by a new team. Naturally, they kept their best players. The NHL wanted the new teams to have a chance to reach the Stanley Cup Finals, though. So they put the new teams in one group and the old teams in another. The winner of each group would then meet in the Finals. When Montreal met St. Louis in the Finals, they thought winning the Cup would be easy. However, St. Louis had several players who had played for Montreal before and knew the team's weak spots. Each game was close, decided by only one goal. Though Montreal took the Cup in four games straight, St. Louis forced two games into overtime and Montreal had to push hard for each win.

## Cool Fact!

To make the puck easier to see on television, the surface below the ice is painted white.

## Trouble with WHA

In 1972, the World Hockey Association (WHA) formed. Although the NHL had expanded, the WHA thought more cities would like to have hockey teams. To get top players from the NHL, the WHA offered higher pay. The WHA also challenged a rule, called the reserve clause, that made it difficult for NHL players to leave teams. The rule was changed, and players gained more freedom to switch teams and seek better contracts.

*The WHA had its own championship trophy made— but the Avco Cup wasn't ready for the first championship finals. The winners had to skate around the rink with another trophy!*

## Money Talks...

At a time when the average NHL salary was $25,000, the WHA signed NHL superstar Bobby Hull for a 10-year contract of $2.7 million. The money talked and 66 more players left the NHL for the chance to make more money. They went to the WHA even though they couldn't play for the Stanley Cup there.

*Bobby Hull was a superstar in both the NHL and the WHA. He won a Stanley Cup with Chicago in 1961. In 1966, he became the first NHL player to score more than 50 goals in a season.*

# THE EXPANSION ERA ROCKS

In 1974, the Philadelphia Flyers became the first expansion team to win the Cup—and they did it their way. Philadelphia played a very tough, physical game that intimidated other teams. They got into many fights and spent a record number of minutes sitting in the penalty box.

## A Dynasty Is Born

Philadelphia won the Cup again in 1975. But their reign didn't last long. The very next season, Montreal knocked them off Lord Stanley's throne with their **superior** speed and skill. Even though the games between the two teams were extremely close, Montreal always had the upper hand. Montreal swept the final series, four games to zero. However, the Flyers still left their mark. As Montreal sipped champagne from the Cup, they also licked bruises that had been "hand-delivered" by Philadelphia.

*Right wing Guy Lafleur helped Montreal become a new dynasty in the 1970s. He scored two game-winners in the 1976 Finals. They were his first-ever goals in the Finals.*

## Montreal vs. Boston

The Canadiens' bruises faded and a new dynasty was born. Montreal went on to win four Cups in a row. Along the way, they clashed with Boston. But Boston was no match for Montreal's firepower. In the 1977 Stanley Cup Finals, Montreal outscored Boston 16-6, claiming the Cup by winning four games in a row. The next year, they met in the finals again. Even though Boston won two games, the firepower of Montreal's superstars put them away again. In the 1980s, two other dynasties emerged: the New York Islanders and Edmonton Oilers.

*By winning four Cups in a row, the 1980-83 Islanders joined the NHL's official dynasties. The others were Montreal (four times), Detroit, Edmonton, and Toronto.*

### Cool Fact!

The first season his team won the Cup, Dave "The Hammer" Schultz of the Philadelphia Flyers racked up a record-setting 472 penalty minutes.

*Dave Schultz was a top **enforcer** in the 1970s.*

# NEW DYNASTIES SHINE

In 1979, the WHA folded. Many of its teams and talented young players entered the NHL. This raised the level of play and skill in the league. New dynasties also came together to battle for the Cup.

## Rising to the Top

In the 1980s, the New York Islanders reached the Stanley Cup finals for the first time. They won and became the team to beat, winning the next three Cups, too. No U.S. team had won the Cup three times in a row before, let alone four. The fourth time, the Islanders whipped the Edmonton Oilers in four games straight. The Oilers were shocked. Their high-scoring superstars had never scored so few goals. The Islanders had outplayed, outmuscled, and outhustled the Oilers all series long. The Oilers took the lesson to heart. The next year, they beat the Islanders for the Cup. It was the first time an ex-WHA team ever won the Cup. The Oilers won the Cup four more times over the next six years.

*Denis Potvin, the team captain, helped lead the Islanders in the 1970s and 1980s as they became a dynasty. He won four Stanley Cups with the Islanders and was named the NHL's top defenseman four times.*

## The Great One and The Moose

No two superstars shaped the Edmonton Oilers' dynasty like Wayne Gretzky and Mark "Moose" Messier. Gretzky, "the Great One," set up and scored so many goals that he rewrote the NHL record book. At the same time, Mark Messier led teammates so fearlessly that they rose to play at his level of power.

*When Wayne Gretzky retired in 1999, he held 61 NHL records. Fifteen of them were playoff records.*

*When Mark Messier played for the New York Rangers in 1994, he promised fans a win against the New Jersey Devils in the Stanley Cup semifinals. He kept his word and led the Rangers to take the Cup.*

# ON THE ROAD

There was a time when Lord Stanley's champions had to steal the Cup to show it off to family and friends. And they did. In 1979, Guy Lafleur of the Montreal Canadiens kidnapped the Cup and took it to his hometown of Thurso, Quebec. But when his son filled it with water from a garden hose, he decided to return it. Nowadays, the Cup hits the road to spend one day with each of the winning team's players in his hometown.

## Stanley's Journal

The Stanley Cup is the only pro sports trophy that has a full-time bodyguard. The Keeper of the Cup watches the Cup 24 hours a day, seven days a week. Perhaps that's a good thing. Players have been known to pour milk and cereal in the Cup for breakfast, take the Cup for a dip in a swimming pool, and even drop-kick the Cup like a football. The Keeper of the Cup posts on the Internet a travel journal of where the Cup goes. Hockey fans can follow the Cup and its adventures as it travels from town to town.

## Cool Fact!

The Stanley Cup has visited the Parliament Buildings in Canada, the White House in the United States, and the Kremlin in Russia.

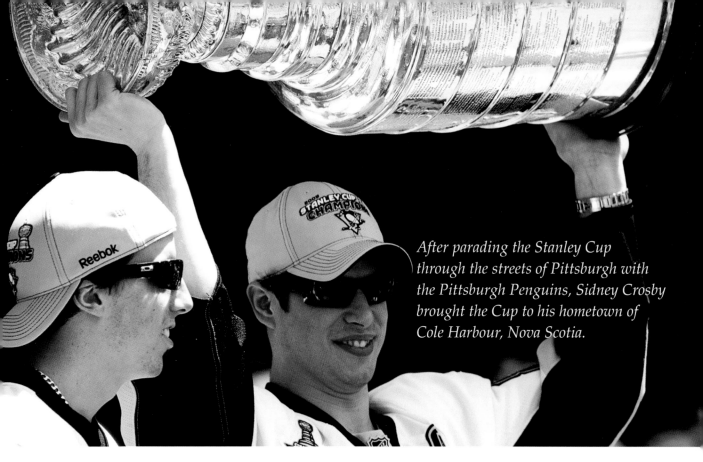

*After parading the Stanley Cup through the streets of Pittsburgh with the Pittsburgh Penguins, Sidney Crosby brought the Cup to his hometown of Cole Harbour, Nova Scotia.*

## Sid the Kid's Day with the Cup

In 2009, Sidney Crosby of the Pittsburgh Penguins brought the Cup to his hometown of Cole Harbour, Nova Scotia. From there, a helicopter flew them to the harbor of the nearby city Halifax. They landed on the flight deck of a battleship and toured the city. Then they returned to Cole Harbour for a parade, where about 75,000 people packed the streets for a glimpse of the Cup.

## Boost for Troops

The Stanley Cup has visited American and Canadian troops in Kandahar, Afghanistan. While overseas, the troops play street hockey to let go of stress and feel more at home. Seeing the Cup up close and having their photos taken with the famous trophy gave their **morale**, or spirit, an awesome boost.

25

Today, teams across North America continue to battle for the Cup. The odds didn't look good for the Los Angeles Kings after the third game in the first round of the 2014 Stanley Cup playoffs. They were down three games to none against the San Jose Sharks. If they didn't win the next four games, they were out of the playoffs.

## Don't Count Us Out

Few teams have ever managed to fight back from being down so many games to win a playoff series. But the Los Angeles Kings were determined to win and they clawed their way out. During two more playoff series, they fell behind in games again, but managed to haul themselves out again to advance to the Stanley Cup finals against the New York Rangers. Five games later, three of which went into overtime, the Kings were the Stanley Cup champions!

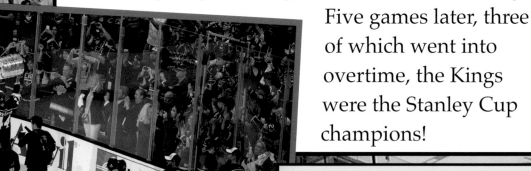

*The Los Angeles Kings took the longest journey ever to win the Cup. They played a record-setting 26 games and won a record number of elimination games.*

## Mr. Game 7

Justin Williams of the Los Angeles Kings won the MVP (Most Valuable Player) award of the 2014 Stanley Cup playoffs. Williams scored 9 goals and racked up 16 assists for a total of 25 points. Five of those points helped his team win do-or-die Game 7s.

*Justin Williams (below) comes through when it counts. In the 2014 playoffs, he set a record for the most career points in Game 7s—14 points in seven games.*

## King of the Net

Fans and teammates don't call him King for nothing. Henrik Lundqvist rules the New York Rangers' net. In the 2014 playoffs, the star goalie stopped 40 or more shots three times in the five-game final series against the Los Angeles Kings. In Game 4 of the series, King's sensational saves won the game for New York.

*Henrik Lundqvist is one of the top goalies in the world. In the 2014 Stanley Cup playoffs, he was both a key to the Rangers' success and a tough obstacle for the Kings.*

# THE CLARKSON CUP

What's the Stanley Cup of women's hockey? The Clarkson Cup! Named after Canada's former Governor General Adrienne Clarkson, the trophy is becoming the ultimate prize of women's hockey. It is awarded to the winner of the Canadian National Championship between the Canadian Women's Hockey League and the Western Women's Hockey League.

## Move Over, Stanley

When the NHL season was canceled in 2004-2005 because of a labor dispute between the owners and players, Clarkson suggested that women compete for the Stanley Cup. But not everyone agreed. So she created the Clarkson Cup just for women's hockey. In 2009,

*The Boston Blades won the Clarkson Cup in 2013. They were the second U.S. winner, after Minnesota in 2010.*

the Montreal Stars and Minnesota Whitecaps fought a close game for the first Cup. Tied 1-1, Montreal then scored twice to win the Cup. In 2014, the Toronto Furies met the defending Clarkson Cup champions, the Boston Blades, in the finals. After three scoreless periods, Toronto scored in overtime to win its first Cup.

## Sparkplug on Ice

Caroline Ouellette, a forward, skates for the Canadian National Team and the Montreal Stars. She played college hockey at the University of Minnesota-Duluth and ranks in the top 10 in NCAA scoring. She also won the 2009 and 2010 Clarkson Cup, four Olympic gold medals, and five world championships. That makes her one of just a few women to win **Triple Gold**.

*Caroline Ouellette, nicknamed Caro, was born in 1979. She started playing hockey when she was nine.*

## Scoring Sensation

When Meghan Agosta won the Clarkson Cup in 2012, she became a member of the Triple Gold Club as well. Agosta of the Montreal Stars has a knack for scoring goals. In 2012, she led the CWHL **scoring race**, or most goals scored, and was awarded the Angela James Bowl. One year later, she became the first woman to win the scoring race two years in a row.

*In 2012, Meghan Agosta was awarded the Angela James Bowl. The Angela James Bowl, named for a retired Canadian hockey star, is given to the top points scorer in the Canadian Women's Hockey League.*

# THE FUTURE OF THE STANLEY CUP

Do you dream of skating around the rink with the Cup one day? Or do you just want to play the game for fun? Whatever the case may be, the future of hockey is exciting!

## Get in the Game

You can play hockey in local recreational, community, and school leagues. You can learn hockey skills at little leagues and hockey camps while you have fun playing the game. Tournaments, such as the Junior World Championships, also allow young players to emerge and develop into future superstars who will battle for the Cup. How will you take your first step on the road to the Stanley or Clarkson Cup? Whatever you decide, the most important thing is to get out there and get in the game!

*Attending a hockey camp can improve your game. Remember to have fun and practice hard!*

# LEARNING MORE

Check out these books and websites to find out more about the most coveted prize in sports.

## Books

*The Stanley Cup: All about Pro Hockey's Biggest Event* by Martin Gitlin, Sports Illustrated Kids, 2012

*Inside Hockey: The Legends, Facts, and Feats That Made the Game* by Keltie Thomas, Maple Tree Press, 2008

*The Best of Everything Hockey Book,* by Shane Frederick, Sports Illustrated Kids, 2011

## Websites

**NHL Kids: The Stanley Cup Fun Facts**

This site features many fun facts about the Stanley Cup.
www.nhl.com/kids/subpage/sc_ff.html

**Hockey Hall of Fame: Stanley Cup Journal**

View past and present Stanley Cup Journal.
www.hhof.com/htmlstcjournal/exSCJ_main.shtml

**Stanley Cup Facts and Trivia**

Many interesting facts about the Stanley Cup.
www.kidzworld.com/article/6753-stanley-cup-facts-and-trivia

# GLOSSARY

Note: Some boldfaced words are defined where they appear in the book.

**amateur** Playing a sport without pay

**archrivals** Major or traditional opponents in a sport or game

**axed** Eliminated, got rid of

**body checking** Using the upper arm, hip, or elbow to knock an opponent against the boards or onto the ice, in an attempt to separate the opponent from the puck

**conferences** Groups of sports teams who compete against one another

**Dominion** A self-governing country that was part of the British Commonwealth. Canada was a dominion until 1982, when it became fully independent

**draft** (sports) The process of choosing people, one by one, for sports teams

**enforcer** A hockey player whose main job is to prevent or respond to dirty or violent play by the opposition

**evolved** Developed over time

**folded** Shut down an operation or business, and split up

**Great Depression** A time period during the 1930s when there was worldwide economic hardship. Many people lost their jobs and homes

**grueling** Requiring extreme effort, causing exhaustion

**Stock Market Crash** In 1929, an event when the value of investments fell rapidly and many people lost their life savings

**superior** Greater in quantity or quality

**Triple Gold** A trio of hockey championships, the Stanley or Clarkson Cup, an Olympic gold medal, and a world championship, when won by the same person

**ultimate** Being the greatest of something

# INDEX